ANIMAL COMPANIONS

Karen L. Schmitzpycho

A girl and her dog contemplate swans in this tranquil New Jersey Shore scene, circa 1910.

AN ALBUM OF
ANIMAL COMPANIONS

A COLLECTION OF TURN-OF-THE-CENTURY PHOTOGRAPHS AND EPHEMERA

Karen L. Schnitzspahn

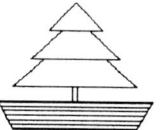

Coast and Pines Press
RED BANK, NEW JERSEY

BOOK DESIGN:
Suzanne Bennett Design, Rumson, New Jersey
PRINTING:
Riverview Press, Little Silver, New Jersey

In Tribute to Wilfred D. Howitt 1919-1995
His artistry inspired me to produce this book.
—*KLS*

Copyright © 1995 by Karen L. Schnitzspahn.
This book, or any portion thereof, may not be reproduced in any form without written permission of the publisher. All rights reserved.
Library of Congress catalog card number:
95-92617

ISBN 0-9649296-0-0

First Edition

Coast & Pines Press
P.O. Box 716
Red Bank, New Jersey 07701

Printed in the United States of America

To:
Tinker, Daisy & Gypsy
Cindy
Caesar & Cleo

TABLE OF CONTENTS

FRONTISPIECE • 2

FOREWORD • 9

INTRODUCTION • 11

DOGS • 16

CATS • 44

HORSES • 50

GOATS & OTHER ANIMALS • 70

TEDDY BEARS • 82

THE PHOTOGRAPHS • 89

THE PHOTOGRAPHERS • 91

THE EPHEMERA • 93

ACKNOWLEDGMENTS • 94

BIBLIOGRAPHY • 95

ABOUT THE AUTHOR • 96

Mrs. Patten and dogs.

LONG BRANCH, CIRCA 1905

FOREWORD

For those of us fortunate enough to have enjoyed that special bond between human and animal companions, Karen L. Schnitzspahn's sojourn back to the turn of the century — where animals had a definite purpose and a very civilized New Jersey Shore community enjoyed society events — will be a truly special treat.

For the reader who has never had the pleasure to explore and experience a quiet walk through fields and hidden trails with man's best friend, these photographs from the Pach New Jersey Shore Collection will, I am sure, be inspiring. Perhaps the book will stir the desire to share life with an animal companion. Or the reader may just want to browse, turning page after page, going back in time for pure enjoyment.

In 1868, Henry Bergh, known as "The Great Meddler," founded the ASPCA in New York City, the first humane society in the Western Hemisphere. Animals had won the right to be protected from cruel treatment and abuse. They grew in status from being just "working animals" to house pets or animal companions.

Who would not agree in looking at this collection of images of children and adults dressed in their best Sunday attire, that happy, well-cared-for dogs and other pets shared family life in exchange for unconditional love or perhaps protection. Elegant, well-groomed horses competed against one another in horse shows while owners looked on with proud expectations. Or, horses just did their part, pulling a carriage or a wagon.

Simple pleasures of years gone by at the shore . . . a lifestyle where everyone dressed properly and elegantly . . . even the animals seem to know just how to pose as captured through the eyes of the photographers.

The very thoughtful selection of pictures contained in this book, however, does not merely reflect a time to reminisce about delightful lifestyles of families, children and their animals. We are, page by page, reminded of our responsibility to be stewards for all animals.

As I write this, the many wonderful animal companions of my childhood and my loyal canine and feline friends presently sharing my life come to mind. What wonderful rewarding moments I have enjoyed. What undemanding love and friendship I've received.

I also can't help but think of the thousands of animals that arrive at animal shelters throughout the country every day of the year. Unwanted, once promised a caring home, they cannot understand why they are no longer wanted. Thousands suffer in silence at laboratories often just for a new and improved cosmetic product.

Today, just as during those wonderful earlier years, animals need our love, protection, and kindness. They still work for us assisting the disabled in so many ways, for example, as hearing aid dogs, guide dogs for the blind, and companions for the wheelchair bound.

Perhaps in our busy, complicated lives we need to take time to keep the promise of our ancestors to let animals share our world and be part of our everyday family life. That playful innocence of our animal companions can still be shared and enjoyed. You will be rewarded with unconditional love.

Animal Companions reflects kindness and consideration for animal life, and the moral and ethical qualities of days gone by.

URSULA GOETZ
Executive Director
Monmouth County SPCA
August 1995

T*he Monmouth County SPCA was incorporated in 1945 and is the local chapter of the New Jersey Society for the Prevention of Cruelty to Animals in Monmouth County, New Jersey.*

A group of foresighted individuals who believed that to be fully human was to be humane established the shelter and found homes for animals. Today the services have expanded to visiting nursing homes with pets, school and community education programs, lost and found assistance and a low cost spay/neuter clinic.

The Monmouth County SPCA is a nonprofit organization, led by a volunteer board of trustees, and supported solely by donations and modest service fees.

Miss Barbour and companions.

CIRCA 1902

INTRODUCTION

Even as a child, I loved to look at old photographs. My grandmother kept albums and a desk drawer stuffed full of memories. The times when she showed me her photographs remain as precious recollections of my childhood. Although faded and torn, the black and white or sepia images possessed a magical quality. Looking at those faces from the past transported me back in time.

Unfortunately, many once-cherished keepsakes of bygone days are thoughtlessly discarded or lost over the years. Today, I own but a few photos of my ancestors. However, I strive to preserve the past, especially the early years of the twentieth century, and those images of families and places that might otherwise be lost forever.

My interests in history and in the art of photography stimulate my efforts to preserve old photographs. Past images provide invaluable details about the way things were. As someone who enjoys taking photographs, I can learn much about artistic photographic techniques by observing early images. Both amateurs and professionals can benefit by studying the methods used in the past. In the pioneer years of photography, the ability of the photographer was more important than the camera and equipment.

As a result of our common interests in history and photography, I had the pleasure of working with George H. Moss, Jr. as co-author of the book, *Those Innocent Years, 1898-1914, Images from the Pach Collection of the Jersey Shore* (Ploughshare Press, 1993). Through that experience, I gained an even greater appreciation of early portraiture, especially the work of Pach photographers Gustavus W. Pach and George A.M. Morris.

While working on *Those Innocent Years,* I was fortunate to find some long lost glass negatives of portraits from the Pach collection of the New Jersey Shore through an antique dealer. I worked diligently to clean up the negatives and to make contact prints of the images, most of which had not even been seen for decades. My favorite photos were of people with their animal companions. Thus, I came up with the idea of compiling these images in one volume showcasing only those pictures that featured animals. Also, I included photographs from the main body of the Pach Jersey Shore Collection belonging to the Moss Archives, using a few that already appeared in *Those Innocent Years.* By careful selection and editing, I documented animal companions of the era highlighting the relationships between those animals and the people in the photos as seen through the eyes of the Pach photographers. I also added various ephemera including postcards, advertisements, and amateur snapshots to give a more detailed look back at animal companions of the era.

Choosing the images proved to be a difficult but enjoyable challenge. As I would hold dusty glass negatives up to the light, viewing them for my first time, I found certain images to be particularly appealing. The way that a little girl in a delicate, lacy frock would allow her small dog to sit on her lap and how the dog sat so placidly for the photographer made an impression on me. The sleek, well-defined lines evident in a portrait of a woman on her horse gave me a sense of grace and elegance and emphasized the importance of horses for sport and leisure. A photo of a boy in a floppy hat proudly driving an express wagon hitched to a goat team lifted my spirits with a feeling for the fun children and animals experienced together in those days. In one of my favorite images from this collection, a cat entered the scene and blended in on the table next to a china tea set belonging to the daughter of photographer G.W. Pach. Perhaps the fact that Pach continued right on taking the photographs with the unexpected cat illustrates the acceptance of animal companions as part of the household during the era.

Professional photographers often produced images of popular animal companions such as dogs, cats, ponies, and goats. Favorite pets played prominent roles in family portraits. Clients would either go to the studio for a sitting, bringing their animal companions with them, or photographers would travel to their homes or places of business to take portraits on location. During the years represented in this collection, The Pach Brothers' New Jersey Shore firm operated studios on Brighton Avenue in the West End section of Long Branch, a popular summer seaside resort, and on Clifton Avenue in Lakewood, a thriving inland winter resort.

For this book, I have used the word companion to denote a variety of household pets, some animals raised for sport treated with love and respect, and a few working animals handled as companions by their owners and not merely as workers. To a privileged few during this era, perhaps certain pets merely satisfied a decorative or ornamental purpose, but most of the animals seen in these photos represent well-respected family members.

Some animals served as mascots for various groups while others were employed as workers to pull fire trucks, delivery wagons, or street watering vehicles (used to water down the dusty, dry dirt roads). Some of these working animals served as subjects for professional portrait photographers from time to time.

Photographic images of animals abounded in the earliest days of photography. The beginning of American photography is usually considered to be 1839 when Daguerre's exciting invention came to the United States from France. Collectors now treasure antique animal portraits, once common in the early days of photography.

Animals have been the subjects of artists throughout history. For example, animals appeared in ancient Greek and Egyptian art, on Medieval European tapestries, and in nineteenth century paintings by French impressionists including Renoir and Degas. At first, in early civilizations, artists represented animals mostly as deities and then hunters or objects of the hunt. By the eighteenth century, painters and sculptors began to depict more household companions. Sir Edwin H. Landseer, a nineteenth century English artist, is well known for his poignant paintings of companion animals.

The trend toward petkeeping as a bourgeoisie practice gained increased popularity in nineteenth century Europe, particularly in France. Previously, animals were thought of mainly as workers, herders, or hunting companions. In nineteenth century America, most animals served similar functions. Some horses pulled plows on farms; others transported the wealthy in stylish carriages.

The turn of the century brought changes in lifestyles and advances in technology resulting in more leisure time and consequently more opportunities to enjoy caring for pets. The first decade of the twentieth century represented a period of political and social reform called the Progressive Era, but many animals were still being neglected and treated poorly, particularly working animals in the cities.

Although faith in the trusty horse diminished by this time, some people believed the working animal would never would lose its importance. Of course, the automobile did eventually replace the horse. At first, automobiling was a frivolous sport, a novelty for the wealthy to enjoy. Eventually, the increased speed, lowered costs and efficiency of the automobiles became so appealing that, by the 1920s at the New Jersey Shore, horses were associated more with recreational activities than with work, although horses continued to haul wagons for small businesses and pull plows in rural areas.

During the years immediately following the Civil War, entrepreneurs promoted horse racing to lure visitors to the New Jersey Shore. Monmouth Park racetrack opened in 1870, but, in 1893, New Jersey passed anti-gambling legislation forcing Monmouth

Park to close down which hurt the tourist trade in the area. However, around this time, horse shows gained in popularity and attracted large crowds. The Hollywood Horse Show on the grounds of the former Hoey estate in Long Branch, the Rumson Horse Show, and others received a great deal of publicity. Other sports involving horses including riding to the hounds and polo also gained more recognition at this time.

The sporting life dominated the social agendas of the well-to-do crowd who vacationed at the New Jersey Shore. Among the notable families photographed by the Pach firm were the Colliers of publishing fame and the George Jay Gould family (George was the son of notorious financier Jay Gould.) Peter Fenelon Collier started the Monmouth County Hunt in 1885 in Eatontown and later maintained a country estate at Wickatunk in the Marlboro hills. When Peter died, Robert carried on the tradition but his interest in the emerging field of aviation surpassed his interest in the horses and hounds. The tradition of the hunt continues today. However, the object is no longer to catch a fox but merely to chase it.

The family of George J. Gould enjoyed both house pets and horses at Georgian Court, their estate in Lakewood. Riding to the hounds and polo were popular sports with the Goulds. There was a large stable, and the horses owned by Gould were apparently treated quite well but they were mainly kept as instruments of sport.

Although the same degree of cruelty did not exist as in earlier times, there were abuses of animals and particularly of horses during this era. Rachel Lynch, wife of Lakewood businessman Jasper Lynch, crusaded for the fair treatment of animals. Mrs. Lynch did much to see that horses were treated well, and she instituted campaigns to give blankets for horses at Christmas. She protested the use of live targets at recreational shooting meets. Many other society women of the era donated much of their time and money to helping animals and recognizing the need for animal welfare and reform.

During the first decade of the twentieth century, dog shows were gaining in popularity for both participants and spectators. Many summer cottagers at the shore brought their purebred dogs along and enjoyed entering them in competitions. According to The New York Times, August 8, 1909, "Every person along the Jersey Coast, from the Highlands to Point Pleasant, who possesses a dog or has the slightest love for one was present today . . . at the second annual show of the Monmouth County Kennel Club, held at Hollywood Park (Long Branch)." Over the years, many changes have taken place in the requirements for show dogs. Improved nutrition and better grooming supplies have upgraded standards.

Certain dogs were considered fashionable and just as styles in clothing change, the fashion in dogs went through changes. The Dachshund was a favorite breed around 1900 and another well-liked dog at the turn of the century, the Pug, was considered gentle, clean, and intelligent. In the 1890s, one of the most popular dogs in America was the Newfoundland. In *Our Times* (Charles Scribner's Sons, 1927) author Mark Sullivan wrote: "Was there ever a finer animal than the Newfoundland, prized, among other reasons for gentleness with children? In 1900, and during some years before, he guarded nearly every porch door, dozed on almost every hearthstone." By 1925, very few were to be seen. Many breeds of dogs that were unheard of for years are now popular again today.

All dogs were not show dogs. In *Our Times*, Sullivan includes a photo of a boy with a dog and caption, "The dog that had the longest and greatest vogue of all, the mongrel; and the truest of dog-lovers, the American boy." Some dogs provided protection as watchdogs for both homes and businesses before burglar alarms were available. Even though there was not the volume of crime we know today, there were many robberies and people were concerned about their valuables. And other ways that animals could help man were developing. Although seeing eye dogs were not formally trained in America until the 1920s, dogs in the early years of the century no doubt helped disabled people in many ways. By the turn of the century, canine companions were being used for police work and by the military.

Dogs and horses were not the only popular companions. Cats appeared as romanticized animals in art, literature, and advertising from the mid-nineteenth and throughout the twentieth century. The cat has always been considered a mysterious and independent animal. Although there were many beloved cats as pets in the years represented in this book, there are very few cat photos in this collection of Pach photographs. Of course, both households and businesses often kept cats as mouse catchers. There were also some cats desired purely for their ornamental value. However, most cats received respect and affection as pets by both wealthy and average families during this time. Perhaps dogs had more status; perhaps cats were simply less willing to sit still for the photographers.

Goats, well-liked family companions, often pulled children's wagons. Contrary to popular belief, goats were not used to trim lawns although sheep were. Many children enjoyed chickens and ducks as backyard pets and gathered eggs as part of their daily chores. Pigs have gained status as enjoyable pets today but were used as living garbage disposers during this era. Other pets such as rabbits, gold fish, birds and some exotic animals were popular but there are few photos of them in this photographic collection.

Everything was not quite as good as it may now seem in these bygone years, even for those families who were well off. There were many diseases without cures. The first anti-rabies vaccine was introduced by Louis Pasteur in the 1880s but was not readily available to most pet owners until the 1920s or later. A handful of dedicated, talented veterinarians practiced in the Monmouth and Ocean County area, mainly making house calls to farms and residences.

In the early years of the century, small local Societies for the Prevention of Cruelty to Animals were operating at the New Jersey Shore and worked as diligently as possible for the welfare of animals. (The Monmouth County SPCA was incorporated in 1945. See Foreword, page 9). Municipal dog catchers, appointed by local officials, volunteered part time in most towns. Usually, the only solution for animal control was to shoot the diseased or unwanted animals. Overpopulation of animals created problems and many unwanted domestic pets roamed the streets and countryside. There were few leash laws and sanitation was crude.

Commercial pet products were not available as we know them today. Although feed was sold for farms and horses, household pet foods did not appear on the market until the late 1920s. Domestic animals ate table scraps and home prepared foods. Commercial pet foods were not even common in many homes until as late as the 1950s. Items such as saddles, bridles, goat harnesses, and many styles of dog collars were readily available from stores and catalogs. Some people went to great lengths to make their pets comfortable. A 1902 Long Branch newspaper describes plans for building a marvelous new do it yourself doghouse — "A Decorative and Dignified Doghouse for the Garden."

Traveling circuses, vaudeville acts, and wild west shows featured animal acts. There is no doubt that many of these animals were not treated well and suffered a great deal. Nevertheless, managers and trainers claimed they took good care of their animals. Many street and boardwalk entertainers performed at the New Jersey shore including organ grinders with their monkeys. Charity circuses were also popular during this era, and some animals appeared in them although these events often featured people in masks and costumes rather than real animals.

The seeds of awareness that some species of animals could be wiped off the face of the earth started to sprout at this time. Some individuals began to take notice of the plight of vanishing animals such as the passenger pigeon and the buffalo. There were many self-proclaimed naturalists and a general interest in science and animal behavior flourished. People enjoyed visiting museums of natural history and reading books and articles about nature. On the other hand, both local hunting and faraway big game hunting were popular pastimes. Homes were often decorated with specimens of taxidermy and with precious items such as exotic animal skins and ivory.

Both the fur and feather industries exploded because of the trends in fashion during this era. Wealthy people created a tremendous demand for fur to embellish their elegant clothes and the more rare the animal, the more desirable it was. Ostrich plumes and Aigrette feathers adorned fashionable colossal hats. Powder puffs were made from feathers. Most people simply did not think about any problems related to the extravagant uses of these animal products or that their source could ever be depleted. But there were protests and some favorite celebrities of the era spoke out against wearing feathers such as actress Minnie Maddern Fiske who started an anti-feather campaign.

Animal characters proliferated in advertising, theatrical productions, and literature. Popular authors of the day including Jack London and Mark Twain wrote of companion animals. The children's periodicals such as *St. Nicholas* and *Chatterbox* featured stories ranging from cute little tales of ducks and kittens to heroic true-life rescues by animals. Some characters such as "Nana," the St. Bernard in J.M. Barrie's *Peter Pan* have remained well known in various versions of the story throughout the entire twentieth century.

Celebrities enjoyed being photographed with their pets. Theodore Roosevelt (President, 1901- 1909) and his family were well known for their many animal companions including the White House cat, "Slippers." An interesting similarity exists between " Slippers" and President Bill Clinton's cat " Socks" of the 1990's. Many American Presidents kept celebrated pets, perhaps the most famous of all being "Fala," Franklin D. Roosevelt's Scottie.

The last section of photos in this book celebrates a favorite plaything conceived during this era, the teddy bear. A political cartoon by artist Clifford Berryman appeared in 1902 depicting President "Teddy" Roosevelt while on a hunting trip in Mississippi, sparing a bear cub from being shot. Although the original intentions of the cartoon were political, the public seemed to perceive it differently, many believing it showed Roosevelt's love of animals and conservation efforts despite his paradoxical reputation as a big game hunter. Roosevelt strived to preserve and manage our vast tracts of public land.

Soon after the cartoon appeared, a Brooklyn, New York, candy store owner named Morris Mitchom seized the opportunity to design toy bears and began to manufacture them. At the same time, in Germany, a dressmaker named Margrete Steiff originated the world famous "button in the ear" Steiff bears that quickly became popular sellers in America. Bears were "all the rage" during this era and have endured to the present day.

It appears that the Pach studios had some teddy tears available for children to pose with, and some children no doubt brought their favorite stuffed bears along. Although nothing can truly be a substitute for a real animal companion, the toy bears may have helped to stimulate respect for animals in a general way. The overwhelming response to the teddy continues and the bears can be of great comfort to many people who for one reason or another cannot keep a live pet. The teddy bear has become a symbol of gentle love and caring.

The era depicted in this book represents both a time of transformation and a time of American innocence before the World Wars. Many people adhered to morals and manners leftover from the Victorian years but others were ready to be bolder, and more willing to speak up about their concerns. It was a time when people began to act more conspicuously for human rights and for animal rights.

I believe that people of all ages can enjoy the photographs of animal companions in this collection. Some readers may peruse the book just for fun, especially animal lovers! Photographic enthusiasts can study the techniques, clarity and artistry of the images. Historians or researchers may view the photos as a look into a slice of the past at the New Jersey Shore. They may learn what animals were fashionable and gain documentation on not only the trends, but also the relationships between the animals and their owners in that society.

It is my hope that the photos will stimulate an awareness of the joy that people of any era can enjoy from close friendships with those loyal and loving companions, the animals

Karen L. Schnitzspahn
August 1995

A dignified-looking woman, identified only by the name "Freece," and her frisky Springer Spaniel sit for a formal portrait at the Pach studio. Originally a sporting dog, the Springer became a popular household companion.

Long Branch 1901

A family, including two of their dogs, assembles for a relaxed outdoor portrait, circa 1907. Families often commissioned photographers to take group portraits at picnics, clambakes, and other outdoor parties. The location of this photo is unidentified but may be at one of the popular restaurants with picnic grounds that were on the banks of the Shrewsbury River in the Long Branch area.

These circa 1910 images of the Willocks at Lakewood reflect a well-to-do family who truly enjoyed their canine companions.

Striking a casual pose, unusual for this era, Mr. Willock, President of a Pittsburgh steel company, reclines on the lawn and appears to be "cross-examining" Otto, his Boston Terrier.

—*The Boston Terrier, one of the few breeds that began in America, originated in Boston about 1870 and rapidly became one of the most popular pets in the country.*

Mrs. Willock stands staunchly beside her Boston Terrier. The dog's easy demeanor and relaxed sitting position complete a charming studio portrait.

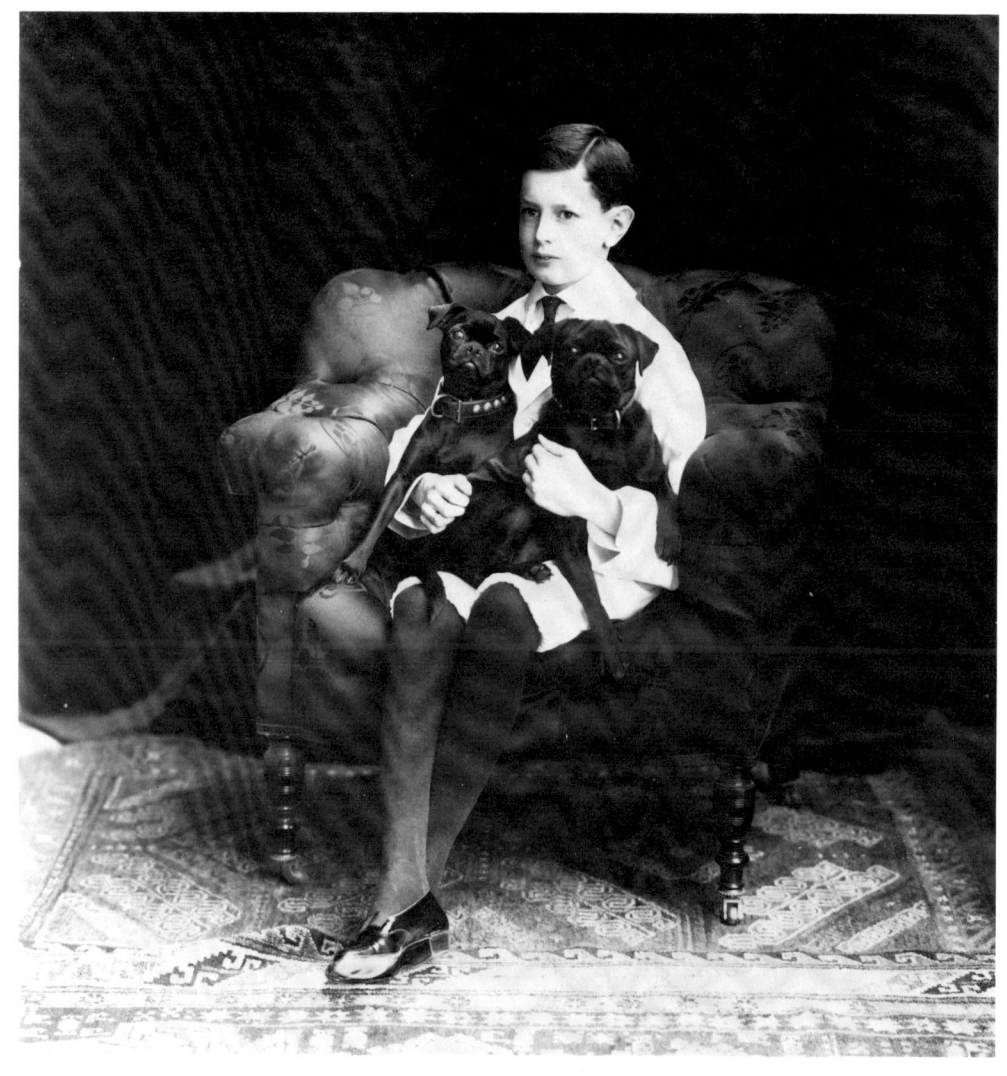

Master Frank Willock proudly holds his two black Pugs as they look with great interest at the camera.

—*The Pug, descended from an ancient Chinese breed, was known as the most popular toy breed in America around the turn of the century but Pomeranians (Poms) and Pekingese (Pekes) soon began to attract even more attention. All three breeds are popular today.*

Mrs. Rhoades instructs her trio of Boston Terriers to look at the camera. The dogs are gazing so attentively at the photographer that one must suspect that he too was giving them a signal. The dog closest to Mrs. Rhoades is "Muggins."

Three members of the Lewisohn family pose wistfully with their dog, most likely a Pekingese. The Lewisohns summered in the Elberon cottage that was previously the home of publisher George Childs and survives today as Stella Maris, a retreat house.

Miss Tilford, in a stylish walking suit and feathered hat, holds the leash of her alert dog, possibly a type of Greyhound. Notice the chic collar that the dog is wearing.

This boy, identified only by the name "Nason," wears a military school uniform. He stands attentively beside his well-behaved French Bulldog, easily recognized by its wonderful bat ears!

—*A French Bulldog is said to be the only animal to perish on the Titanic, the "unsinkable" ocean liner that hit an iceberg and went down in the North Atlantic on April 15, 1912. The dog's owner survived and successfully sued the steamship company for $1,500—a large amount at that time.*

Miss Fordyce gazes at the camera as her splendid Collie looks off to her right.

—*The Collie, once known as the Scottish Shepherd Dog, is a loyal companion, a popular pet both then and now.*

LAKEWOOD, CIRCA 1911

These two boys, whose last name is "Shakespeare," look ready to have some fun. Their Springer Spaniel, usually an active dog, sits peacefully with a more serious expression.

LAKEWOOD, NOV. 29, 1901

Smartly dressed, Miss Blumenthal sits comfortably with her Japanese Spaniel on her lap while a Pach photographer takes their portrait.

—This breed is recognized today by the American Kennel Club as the Japanese Chin.

Even Miss Claire Elgood's marvelous flowered hat cannot take the attention away from her adorable dog, possibly a Maltese Terrier.

Lakewood, 1901

Miss Dorothy Dennis shakes the paw of her loveable canine playmate. This delightful image reflects the essence of companionship with animals and the increasing respect for them during this era.

Lakewood, June 17, 1901

Sunlight peeks through the trees to illuminate the Lawrence baby as he holds his gentle Dachshund.

Circa 1912

Rose Watson and her brother look serious as their Bulldog and Cocker Spaniel occupy the wicker chair. Their Irish Setter and what may be an aging Greyhound (or possibly a smooth Collie) rest peacefully at their feet.

LONG BRANCH, 1902

Dogs often acted as guardians for the estates and cottages at the Jersey Shore.

Dapper John A. McCall looks approvingly at his St. Bernard. This photo is in front of a massive column of "Shadow Lawn," the West Long Branch mansion McCall built in 1903 (see postcard below).

—Shadow Lawn, President Woodrow Wilson's Summer White House of 1916, burned down and in 1927 was replaced by a mansion that is now part of Monmouth University.

Two dogs keep watch in the driveway of the Heisley home in Long Branch while a gentleman wearing a straw boater keeps an eye on them.

CIRCA 1905

Mrs. T. Morse and her delightfully shaggy Old English Sheepdog pose for a photo at a Long Branch dog show in 1911.

—Two Old English Sheepdogs named "Haig" and "Pershing," who helped rescue hundreds of wounded soldiers during World War I, then toured the Unites States to the delight of cheering crowds.

At the same 1911 show as above, Mr. Donnelly stands proudly with his St. Bernard.

—The St. Bernard was originally bred by monks of the Hospice of St. Bernard in the Swiss Alps for the purpose of rescuing travelers during snowstorms.

Rachel Lynch's St. Bernard sports a flowered ribbon. The background reveals a wall of Lynx Hall, the Lynch family's castle-like home in Lakewood depicted in the 1907 postcard insert. Mrs. Lynch crusaded for the fair treatment of animals.

The members of a United States Life Saving Service group, possibly at Monmouth Beach, circa 1899, pose for a portrait while their trusty old canine pal rests in front of them, unbothered by the camera. The dog may not have participated in rescues but was no doubt a comfort to all who did.

—William Augustus Newell, a physician and political figure who lived in western Monmouth County, founded the important service in 1848.

This Norwood baseball team, most likely a summer group of players from various universities, gathers for an informal portrait. The man in front is trying to keep a lively Terrier (probably the team mascot) still.

LONG BRANCH 1898

Mr. and Mrs. Patten gleefully show off their Dachshund, French Poodle, and West Highland Terrier in this outdoor portrait.

Long branch, Circa 1907

Mr. Daly (right), another gentleman, and an Irish Setter look somewhat annoyed at the intruding photographer.

Long Branch, Circa 1905

Dogs enjoyed boating at the Jersey Shore, often providing company for owners of yachts and fishing boats.

In this photograph (photographer unknown), Robert H. Metcalfe, Erskine Hazard and Joseph Rowland pose proudly with "Mac," Metcalfe's dog and unofficial Bay Head Yacht Club mascot.

BAY HEAD 1912

Courtesy Wm. C. Schoettle / Bay Head Yacht Club

A pipe-smoking man, probably a trainer, holds the Beadleston family's dogs, an "English Bull and Pup."

WEST END (LONG BRANCH) 1911

—The Bulldog, one of the oldest of English breeds, was originally developed for fighting bulls, a practice that was outlawed in England by 1835. Although a fearless watchdog, the Bulldog makes a friendly and trustworthy pet.

Looking debonair, Dr. Paul Kimball and a Bulldog companion take a spin around the grounds of Georgian Court (now Georgian Court College), the turn-of-the-century Lakewood estate of millionaire George Jay Gould. Kimball, who had an office in Lakewood, was the Gould family physician. The Kimball Medical Center, Lakewood, is named in his honor.

CIRCA 1905

Latest photograph of MISS LILLIAN RUSSELL and her favorite pet. Miss Russell will appea[r] in a new play, entitled "The Widow's Might." *Photograph by Cross, Chicago.*

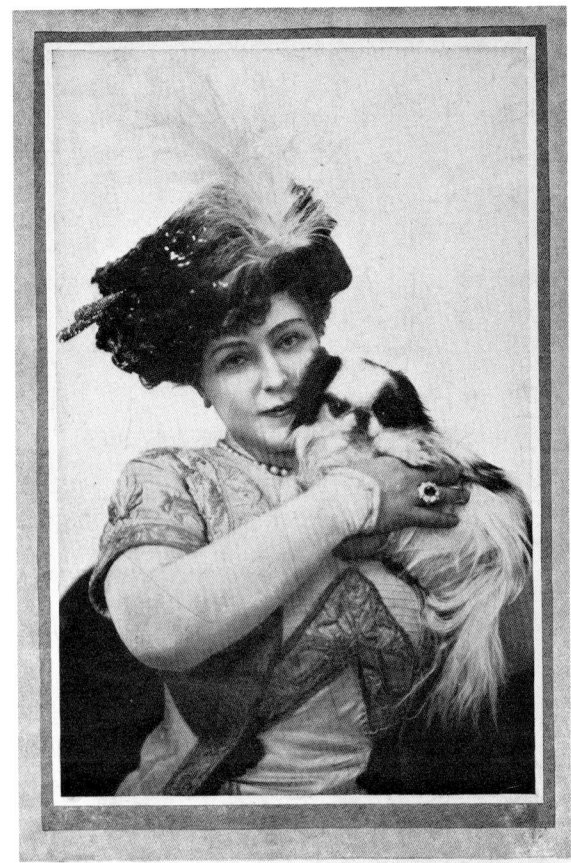

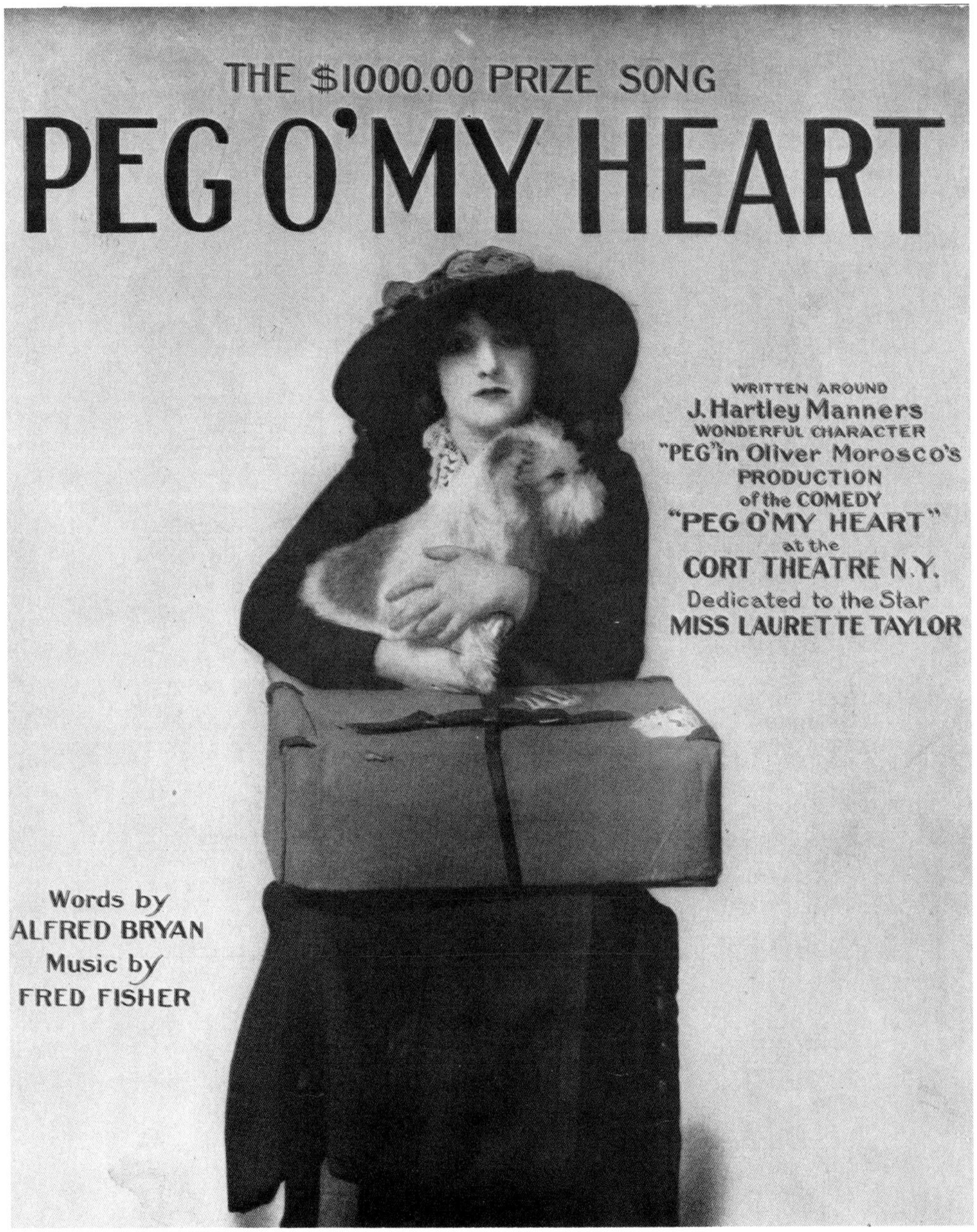

CELEBRITIES AND THEIR DOGS

The legendary entertainer, Lillian Russell, was a frequent visitor to the New Jersey Shore. In this news photo, circa 1910, she is featured with her favorite pet.

Animal companions, both real and people in costumes, appeared in popular shows of the era. "Peg O'My Heart," a Broadway hit of 1912, featured Laurette Taylor with a Terrier as seen on this sheet music.

L. Sisson

Actor John Drew, uncle of Lionel, Ethel, and John Barrymore, is shown on a postcard with one of his dogs. Both the Drews and Barrymores frequented the New Jersey Shore.

P. Hollingsworth

Robert B. Mantell (1854-1928), the notable Shakespearean actor, relaxes with his devoted Fox Terrier, "Rubber." Mantell toured the country extensively and often took his dog with him. This family photo was taken in Mantell's studio at "Brucewood," the actor's home on Avenue D in Atlantic Highlands (The house remains today as the St. Agnes Thrift Shop).

The small photo at the left, circa 1908, is of Mantell, Marie Booth Russell (his third wife), and Rubber at Brucewood. Rubber, at the age of almost fifteen, tragically disappeared in Atlantic Highlands one day in 1913 and was never found.

The images on this page, circa 1900, are family photos, probably taken by Mr. Tilton of Fisher Place, Red Bank. The photos are of people and their pets who lived in the area of Fisher Place on the Navesink River.

Annual Dog Show at Long Branch

Mrs. Foster Rawlins, showing "Midsummer Pyramus" and "Midsummer Thisbe"; a section of the Long Branch Kennels in the background

Miss Ruth Dodd with "Bob"

Mrs. D. Cella with "Falstaff"

Annual Dog Show at Long Branch

Mr. Amsey S. Dodd (right of center) and St. Bernards, with which he won at the show

Miss Dorothy Doran with "Laddie"

H. N. Davis and "Ludhar" of Valley Farms

From a 1917 Long Branch souvenir booklet

The Spaulding's fluffy cat is softly backlighted to create an exquisite feline portrait. This elegant-looking, long-haired cat was probably pampered and allowed to snooze on all the best furniture.

Rumson 1905

Do you detect the difference between these two portraits of Minna Pach, the daughter of photographer G.W. Pach, with her dolls? After Minna serves "tea" in the top photo, her small black cat has entered the scene and sits on the table, almost blending into the picture below. Minna raises her cup to sip some imaginary tea, and her father continues to shoot the photos.

LAKEWOOD 1899

This illustration appeared in the popular children's magazine, St. Nicholas, *in January 1908, depicting President Teddy Roosevelt escorting a group of visiting ambassadors around "Slippers," Roosevelt's legendary six-toed cat. Asserting independence as cats often do, Slippers simply did not want to move out of the way. Jacob A. Riis, the famed journalist, photographer, and social reformer, wrote the story about Slippers that accompanied this picture. The parallel that can be drawn between Slippers' position as the White House family pet and that of President Bill Clinton's cat "Socks" of the 1990s is remarkable!*

"WITH AN AMUSED BOW, THE PRESIDENT ESCORTED THE AMBASSADRESS AROUND 'SLIPPERS,' AND KEPT ON HIS WAY TOWARD THE EAST ROOM."

Calendars during this era often included animal companions. This 1904 "Calendar of the Girl and the Cat" featured captivating art work by Clarence Underwood.

Actor William Gillette is remembered for his role as Sherlock Holmes and for the castle he built as his house in Connecticut. In a photo from The Theatre, *1902, he strokes his favorite cat, a charmer who once made it onto the stage unexpectedly during a performance!*

Miss Horne confidently sits astride her horse, most likely ready for a Monmouth County horse show. Her stylish riding habit reflects elegance and grace.

Circa 1909

—This tail of this handsome horse is cut short or "docked." The purpose of docking, a practice seldom seen today, was to keep the tail from getting caught in carriages, or for a field hunter, to keep thistles from getting caught in the tail.

In this action photo, circa 1909, Miss Horne and Mr. Dwyer are enjoying a ride in the country.

—*Note that Miss Horne is riding sidesaddle as most women traditionally did. Around the turn of the century, more women began to wear split skirts and to ride sitting astride as Miss Horne does for the portrait on the opposite page.*

A Pach photographer captures the moment of a great jump by A.J. Davis and horse at a Monmouth County steeplechase event, circa 1910.

—*Camera shots depicting motion were more difficult to accomplish in the early days as film speeds were slower, and the cameras were more cumbersome.*

Mr. Anthony Brady of Long Branch frequented horse shows in Monmouth County. His handsome pair of perfectly matched horses are hitched up to a bike wagon, a type of runabout.

In front of The New Monmouth Hotel, Spring Lake, Mr. Jones, proudly sits in his speed wagon. His sleek horse with head checked is ready and waiting for the command to begin trotting. Jones may be preparing for a match against a friend.

—*Gentlemen often conducted private races in the streets called matinee races, usually on Sunday afternoons.*

In this charming portrait, baby takes the reins to drive a wicker governess cart. Obviously, the pony chosen for this family had to be gentle. The animal appears healthy, happy, and proud.

—*The diamond pattern on the wicker is an indication of the high quality of the cart.*

By the boardwalk in front of the old West End Casino (Long Branch), two young boys are ready for a fun hayride.

The Halsey children of Rumson are dressed in costumes for a children's parade.

—Ponies and children make great friends and this animal, possibly a Shetland, seems very tolerant. Ponies can live long lives and exhibit great loyalty to a family.

A set of twins and another boy wait in a wagon near a boardwalk at the New Jersey Shore. They are eager to ride as the boy in front of the ponies keeps an eye on the group.

Miss Clark poses formally at a Long Branch horse show in her phaeton, a fashionable carriage for proper ladies of the era.

—*Her horse's head is checked and the animal is meticulously groomed. It was the custom for society people to ensure that their horses' heads were held up high. This was accomplished by using check reins that were not comfortable for the horses as they would be unable to put their heads down. There was no necessity for checking the head, it was purely for fashion or show.*

Looking content, Matt Kahn is out for a leisurely ride on Ocean Ave., Long Branch. The horse's ears are perked and slanted back, listening for Mr. Kahn's next command. Kahn wears attachments over his regular shoes that look like boots but can be taken off easily.

Horses, riders, and hounds prepare for a hunt meet, circa 1905, at Laurel-in-the-Pines. This elegant Lakewood hotel, the site of many social and sporting events, first opened in 1891 and was destroyed by fire in 1967.

This snow scene featuring a Collier hunt group includes publisher Peter Fenelon Collier, third from left, and his son, Robert, far left. At their country home, "Rest Hill" at Wickatunk the Colliers hosted many sporting and social events. Peter established the Monmouth County Hunt in 1885 at Eatontown. Today the Wickatunk (Marlboro Township) estate is the home of Collier Services.

Circa 1905

—Riding to the hounds continues to be popular in New Jersey today, although now the event is a fox chase rather than a fox hunt.

In Lakewood, 1898, George Jay Gould (third from left), family members and friends are ready for the call. The participants gather around one rider who is probably the master of hounds. The birdseye view of Georgian Court, Gould's estate, taken from the tower of the stable, was a Pach photo published by a postcard company.

This portrait of financier George Jay Gould captures him on a favorite polo pony. Gould holds his mallet and looks directly toward the camera with an expression of serious determination. The two postcards depict Gould polo matches at Lakewood.

—Polo has been called the fastest team game in the world. Polo ponies are alert, quick and agile as they often have to stop and turn on a dime and then sprint from a standstill. The polo pony's mane is "roached" or cut to keep it from getting in the way of the player's hands.

Wearing a clown costume and ready to have some fun at a charity circus, circa 1905, Howard S. Borden of Rumson, a businessman and sportsman known as "General Borden," drives his tandem gig.

— This type of cart is usually pulled by two horses, one in front of the other, but for this event a solitary horse dressed in human clothing does the job.

No, this is not the real Buffalo Bill Cody, although the legendary showman did have ties with the New Jersey Shore. Standing beside a dark horse (B.B. traditionally rode a white horse), A.J. Byrne impersonates Buffalo Bill for the Deal amateur circus, 1908.

The West End (Long Branch) Hose Company poses proudly in front of the boardwalk in 1912. Apparently, they have won a trophy in a competition.

—The horses are fine working animals. Fire horses were traditionally white. The Company's Dalmatian exhibits great trust by standing at the feet of the horses. Dalmatians have a history as coach dogs who would trot alongside the horses and even sleep in the stables with them. Dalmatians also make good-natured household companions and are known to be courageous and loyal.

The Hollywood Horse Show Grounds, in the West End section of Long Branch, bustled with excitement as evidenced in this 1909 photo.

The Famous Long Branch Horse Show

Judging Saddle Horses

THE LONG BRANCH HORSE SHOW, an annual event the last week in July, has for more than two decades been acknowledged the greatest open air show in America. Its promoters and exhibitors have been, and are, the leaders in this field of sport. Its entries, numbering upwards of 700, constitute the finest showing made annually in this country. It has sixty classes, and trophies costing $8,000; and finally, most important of all from a spectacular stand-point, a very large following of the leaders of American society. Social functions of Horse Show Week (private and public), large garden fetes and horse show balls, receptions and teas, approach a carnival. Grounds of the Long Branch Horse Show Association cover twenty-five acres and are most amply equipped

The Famous Long Branch Horse Show

A prize-winner, four-in-hand, exhibited by Hamilton Farm

HORSE RACING is a minor but popular feature of the show, generally being the final event of each afternoon's program

The gallery awaiting the bugle call at the Annual Horse Show of the Monmouth County Association

From a 1917 Long Branch souvenir booklet.

The amateur snapshots on this page are from a family album belonging to a Little Silver or Long Branch family, name unknown. Handwritten captions on backs of photos read clockwise from top left as follows: "Sunday morning just after having crossed the big bridge (Little Silver) Sept. 1900;" "Mr. T., Sunday morning, August 27, 1901;" "Peaches with Jaxseed...and Fred Morris, Sept. 1900;" "Peaches and Lee just a few days before our dear horse died, Sept. 23, death, 1900."

What could have brought these eight horses together to pose for this remarkable photograph, circa 1905? It is rare for horses to form such a line and especially to stay like this for a photo.

Two goats pull the Fisk boy's "Favorite" wagon on a sunny, carefree day.

—Goat carts prevailed as popular toys from the mid-nineteenth century through the first two decades of the twentieth century.

WEST END 1905

A pet goat leads a baby and his nurse for a walk on a brisk winter's day.

LAKEWOOD, CIRCA 1915

Ready for the 1901 Asbury Park Baby Parade and Children's Carnival, this delightful group poses in the Pach studio with a patriotic goat cart.

—*The Baby Parades held on the Asbury Park boardwalk began in 1890 and continued for many years becoming increasingly elaborate and reaching their peak in the 1920s. Many costumes and floats incorporated children's pets.*

This "Watson" group of men in Scottish garb are driving a wagon pulled by two handsome goats wearing plaid ribbons. The photo was taken on the Rumson side of the Sea Bright Bridge, circa 1902.

In this captivating studio portrait, is Alfred Woehr telling his kid to "Stay" or simply reminding his pet not to be naughty?

Lakewood, March 27, 1899

Two toddlers feed a gentle goat. Few words are needed to describe the trusting relationship between children and animals reflected in this image.

LAKEWOOD, CIRCA 1915

Wearing a wonderful hat, sporting a curl in the middle of his forehead, and proudly holding his pet guinea pig, this child happily poses for a portrait, circa 1902.

— Although many guinea pigs were used for medical laboratory experiments during this era, some guinea pigs served only as friendly companions for children.

"Kemp's Sheep"—These sheep graze at the Kemp Rumson Hill estate that became the McCarter property after Kemp's death in 1900. Kemp, a businessman, enjoyed farming and introduced Holstein and Guernsey cows to the shore area. Sheep helped to trim lawns. Contrary to popular belief, goats were not usually used for this purpose.

—During the First World War, President Woodrow Wilson kept sheep on the White House Lawn in Washington DC during the absence of the gardeners who were overseas.

In a 1900 amateur photo, cows graze contentedly in a Little Silver meadow that is now probably a busy residential neighborhood.

These candid photos of boys feeding chickens were taken by Pach photographer Alfred J. Meyer of Long Branch.

—Meyer gained recognition for his pictures of President Theodore Roosevelt and family.

Chickens and ducks were common backyard pets during this era. The chicken in the top photo may be a Barred Plymouth Rock and below are Leghorns.

In this charming image, providing a study in textures, a baby contemplates two parakeets.

Lakewood, Circa 1915

—Although pet birds were prevalent in the early twentieth century and are enjoyed today, their popularity seemed to reach a peak in the Victorian era. The 1889 diary of a summer visitor to a Long Branch hotel states that she arrived with two trunks and eight bird cages!

On a porch of the Darlington Inn, a waitress tries to gently coax a pet monkey to pay attention to her. One can only speculate about the reason for the bandage that is visible on one of the woman's fingers.

DARLINGTON (DEAL BEACH) 1900

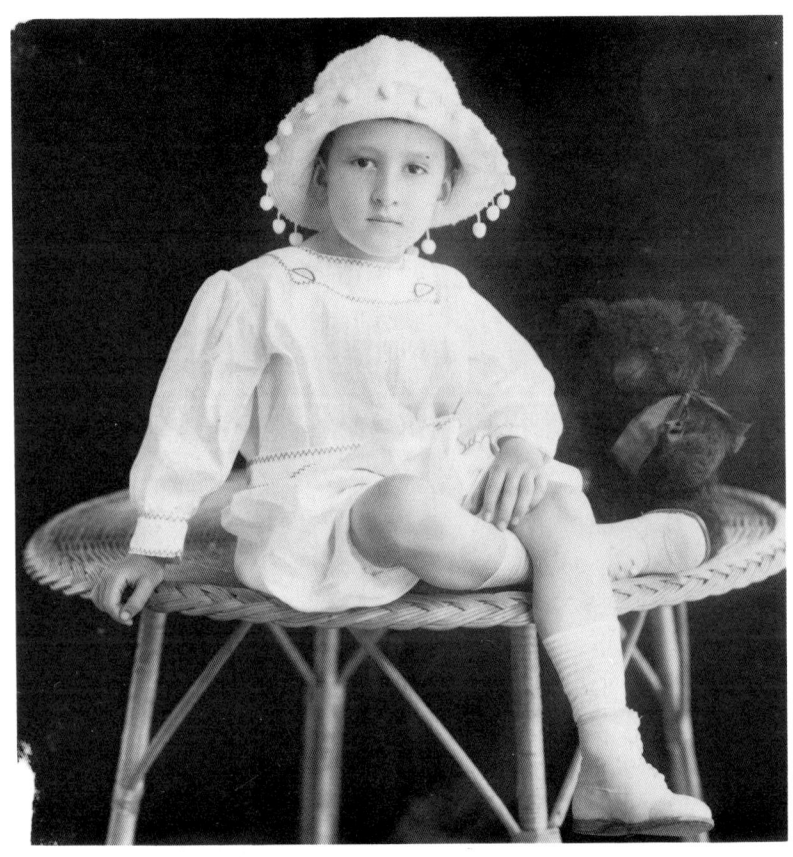

"Master Willock," circa 1905, wears a wonderful hat decorated with pom poms. Sitting on the wicker table next to him is a charming dark, fluffy, and unusual teddy. This may be the same Master Frank Willock on page 21, a few years earlier.

Mrs. Stewart Duncan's baby interacts with a large teddy bear in this adorable portrait.

In this winsome 1905 image of the Schauffler child of Lakewood, a teddy bear sits by her foot.

Dressed in matching hats and sweaters and knee pants, the Barbour brothers, with a teddy bear at their feet, pose for a portrait in Lakewood.

—*In both of these photographs, the children and teddy bears seem to be detached but complement one another to make the portraits more interesting.*

The Landsburgh child, circa 1912, smiles and looks happy to be sitting with a congenial, large teddy bear companion.

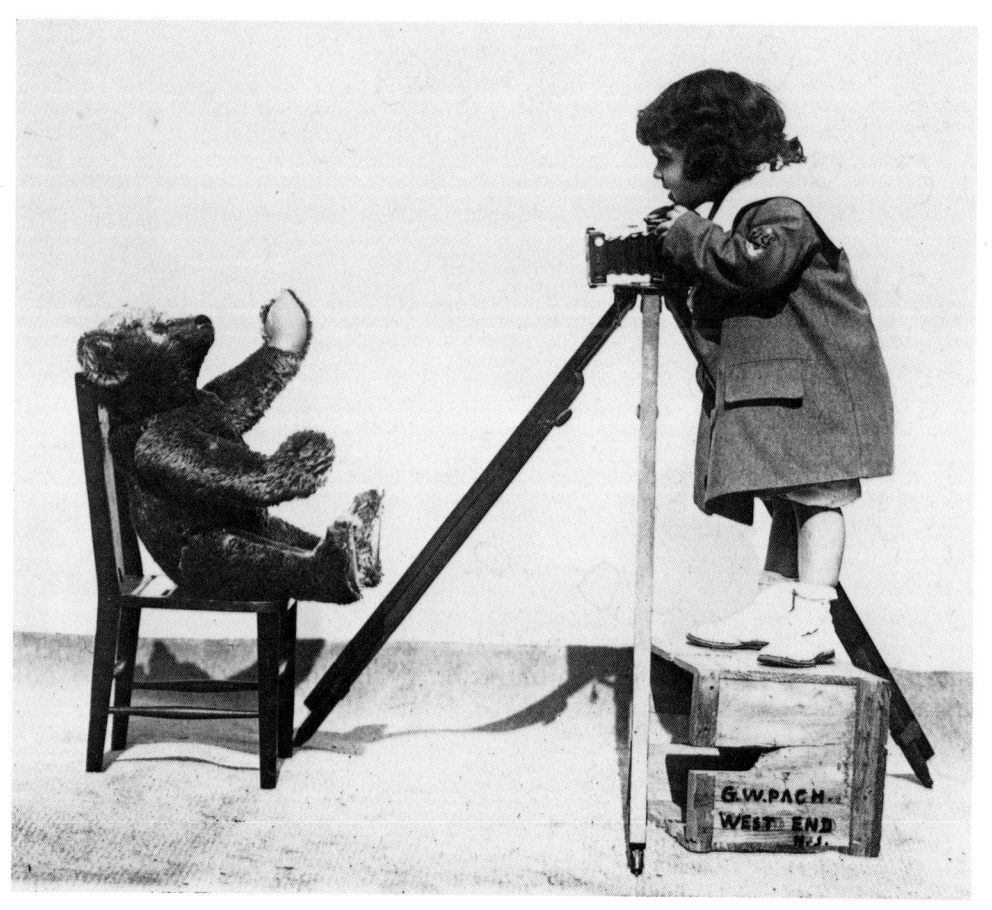

Young John Conklin plays photographer with a studio teddy as his model. This photo may have been intended as an advertisement for Pach Brothers.

THE PHOTOGRAPHS

Most of the illustrations in this book are either from the author's collection or The Moss Archives, Sea Bright, New Jersey. The photographs are unretouched contact prints made from glass negatives taken (1898-1914) by the New Jersey Pach Brothers firm and (around 1915) by George A.M. Morris.

To present the images in the format needed for this volume, photos are cropped, reduced, or enlarged. Some defects from age may be seen in the images although their clarity and detail remain.

The names of people and pets, breeds of animals, and locations of the photos are identified as much as possible. Dates are given specifically in the captions whenever known. Some photos are "circa" if an exact date could not be determined. Many of these delightful images have not been seen since they were first taken over eighty years ago. Several of them appeared in *Those Innocent Years* by Moss and Schnitzspahn, Ploughshare Press, 1993.

The Pach photographic wagon, 1905

THE PHOTOGRAPHERS

The Pach photographers responsible for most of these images are Gustavus W. Pach and George A.M. Morris. The history of the Pach Brothers firm goes back to the summer of 1866 in Long Branch, New Jersey, a seaside resort that lured the rich and famous from New York and Philadelphia. Gustavus W. Pach and his younger brother, Gotthelf, were working out of a cigar store in Long Branch, taking orders for photographs and using a horse-drawn wagon as a mobile studio. As the story goes, the Pach brothers were sent on assignment to the lavish summer cottage of Philadelphia publisher, George W. Childs.

Childs introduced the aspiring photographers to his friends, financier Anthony Drexel and the illustrious General Ulysses S. Grant. Impressed by the Pach brothers hardworking manner, Grant convinced Childs and Drexel to contribute cash to the photographers so they could start their own business. In 1867, the Pach brothers opened their first studio at Long Branch.

After Grant was elected President in 1869, his Long Branch summer cottage at Elberon became "The Summer White House," and the popularity of the resort increased. Consequently, the Pach's business flourished.

The Pachs soon established additional studios. They were running successful enterprises at the New Jersey Shore but wanted to maintain a year-round clientele, and, in 1868, opened a studio in New York City. Pach Brothers photographed many celebrities, eventually including every chief executive from U.S. Grant to Richard M. Nixon, earning them the title of "Photographers to the Presidents."

Pach Brothers produced many stereographic views of the New Jersey Shore from 1868-1885 (documented in *Double Exposure Two* by George H. Moss, Jr., Ploughshare Press, 1995) and scenes for postcard publishers as the postcard became popular around the turn of the century.

In 1896, Pach Brothers opened a studio in Lakewood, New Jersey, on Clifton Avenue. Lakewood, a fashionable "winter paradise" attracted wealthy families and provided an ideal site for a photographic business to prosper. Encircled by a pine forest and less than ten miles inland from Barnegat Bay, Lakewood boasted mild weather and splendid hotels.

Pach Brothers also operated branch studios at strategic locations in university towns. They were taking photographs for Harvard, Yale, West Point, Princeton, and other schools. At Princeton, New Jersey, in the late 1890s, G.W. Pach met George A.M. Morris and hired him as an apprentice. Morris began his photographic career at Pach's Lakewood studio in 1898. He learned quickly and customers, including magnate George J. Gould, soon requested the talented Morris.

In 1903, Gustavus W. Pach retired from the New York operation and bought out the New Jersey studios. The New York firm continued to prosper for many years until the close of the business in 1993. After G.W. Pach died in 1904, George A.M. Morris ran the New Jersey Shore firm that continued under the name "Pach Brothers" until about 1914. Morris continued to work as a photographer under his own name until his death in 1948 in Long Branch. His son, George Jay Morris, was also a photographer.

The artistry of Pach and Morris is evident in this assortment of photographs featuring portraits of people with their animal companions. The legacy of the Pach Brothers' work lives on.

(A complete, detailed history of "The Pach Photographers" appears in *Those Innocent Years*.)

THE EPHEMERA

The chapter title pages and some additional pages display various ephemera spanning the years from about 1885 to 1920. These items provide extra information regarding animal companions to complement the collection of Pach photographs. Items include postcards, advertisements, newspaper clippings, programs, and amateur family snapshots. It was a common practice from the Victorian years to the 1920s for individuals to keep elaborate scrapbooks and albums. These pages are in keeping with that tradition.

Page 51—The little girl in the center on a horse is Reba Stryker Miller, circa 1905, Marlboro Township; page 82—photo by K.L.Schnitzspahn (1994) of teddy bear and vintage baby shoes; page 83—Boy sitting on bear is W.H. Borden, Rumson, 1918; ad for teddy bears is from Sears Roebuck 1908 catalog.

THE EVENING PRAYER.
A Photograph from real life.
There is a Dog who loves his little master so,
He always goes with him wherever he may go,
And even when he kneels to say his Evening Prayer,
This faithful friend is by his bedside there.

ACKNOWLEDGMENTS

Sincere thanks to George H. Moss, Jr. for allowing me to use items from the Moss Archives, for sharing his wisdom on book production and photography, and most of all for his friendship.

Thanks are due to: Laura Kent Hower and George Hower (Applewood Antiques, Red Bank, NJ) and Autumn Hower; Chris Myer (Shore Antiques Center, Point Pleasant Beach, NJ); The Monmouth County SPCA - Ursula Goetz for her Foreword, my dear friend Nancy Giles, Dennis Bailey, and the SPCA staff; Fran Deiss, The Monmouth County Kennel Club; The American Kennel Club, New York; Dr. R. Yacowitz, DVM, Little Silver Animal Hospital and staff; Michael J. Renehan, the Monmouth County Hunt; Kerry Roemer; Joe Jennings; Edith Borden; Randall Gabrielan; Reba Miller; Peggy Hollingsworth and Laurie Sisson; Ambrose Hardwick Jr.; and Thomas J. Hoffman.

Also, thanks to my parents, Doug and Kari Hunt, for bringing me up to appreciate books, art, theater, and animals. Special thanks to my wonderful sons, Doug and Greg, for their editorial comments and to my husband, Leon, who has given both computer assistance and loving support throughout this project.

Rose Watson and Cocker Spaniel, 1902

BIBLIOGRAPHY

BOOKS:

Belanger, Jerry, *Raising Milk Goats the Modern Way*, Storey Communications, Inc., Pownat, Vermont, 1990.

Berkowitz Mona, *How to Raise and Train an Old English Sheepdog*, T.F.H. Publications, 1967.

Bielfeld, *Guinea Pigs*, Barron's Educational Series, Inc., 1983.

Boyd, Sunni, *Animal Rights*, Lucent Books Inc., San Diego, CA, 1990.

Brewer, Kim and Waugh, Carol-Lynn Rossel, *Antique and Modern Teddy Bears*, Random House, New York, 1990.

Burt, Olive W., *The Horse in America*, The John Day Company, New York, 1975.

Clark, Kenneth, *Animals and Men*, Wm. Morrow and Co., New York, 1977.

Doughty, Robin W., *Feather Fashions and Bird Preservation*, University of California Press, 1975.

Edwards, E.H. & Geddes, C., Eds., *The Complete Horse Book*, Trafalgar Square Inc., North Pomfret, Vermont, 1988.

Encyclopedia Americana, Grolier, 1993.

Gebhardt, Richard C., *The Complete Cat Book*, Howell Book House, New York, 1991.

Hutchinson's Dog Encyclopedia, 1929.

Kelly, Niall, *Presidential Pets,* Abbeville Press, New York, London, Paris, 1992.

Kete, Kathleen, *The Beast in the Boudoir*, University of California Press, 1994.

Lawson, James Gilchrist, *The Book of Dogs*, Rand McNally & Company, Chicago, 1934.

Loeper, John J., *Crusade for Kindness*, Henry Bergh and the ASPCA, Atheneum, New York, 1991.

Moss, G.H., and Schnitzspahn, K.L., *Those Innocent Years, 1898-1914, Images of the Jersey Shore from the Pach Photographic Collection* Ploughshare Press, Sea Bright, NJ, 1993.

Silverman, Ruth, ed., *The Dog Observed*, Photographs 1844-1983, Alfred A. Knopf, New York, 1984.

Sullivan, Mark, *Our Times, The Turn of the Century,* Vol I, Scribner's, New York, 1927.

Wilcox, Bonnie, DVM, and Walkowicz, Chris, *The American Kennel Club, Atlas of Dog Breeds*, 1991.

PERIODICALS:

Animal Protection (SPCA Annual Reports), *Asbury Park Press, Long Branch Daily Record, The New York Times, St. Nicholas, The Red Bank Daily Register, The Theater,* miscellaneous letters, pamphlets, programs, advertisements, and personal interviews.

ABOUT THE AUTHOR

Karen L. Schnitzspahn's diverse interests include the New Jersey Shore during the Victorian era, pioneer photography, the history of the American theatre, and the art of puppetry. She is co-author of *Those Innocent Years, 1898-1914, Images of the Jersey Shore from the Pach Photographic Collection,* and a guest writer for the *Asbury Park Press* column, "A Look Back, A Historical Vignette." Her articles and essays have appeared in regional and national publications, and she has served as writer, designer and consultant for educational programs. Karen is a native of New Jersey and a long-time resident of Monmouth County.

The author and "Danny"
CIRCA 1950